Whispers in Blue

Soumya Varma

 BookLeaf Publishing

Presentation by *BookLeaf Publishing*

Web: www.bookleafpub.com

E-mail: info@bookleafpub.com

ISBN: 9789358738346

First edition 2023

This book is dedicated to my Grade 9 English Teacher Ms. Senthil Vadivu, whose surprise writing challenge got me to write my first ever poem. I hope this book reaches you...

ACKNOWLEDGEMENT

To my mum, dad and sis, you have been my rock and my biggest cheerleaders.

To my husband, thank you for encouraging me in all my pursuits.

To my dearest son, your belief in me has been a constant source of inspiration.

To my friend Vandana, for without you, these words would remain mere thoughts, unshared with the world.

To my family and friends, your conversations and laughter have been the fuel for my creative spirit.

PREFACE

In the intimate pages that follow, you will embark on a journey into the depths of the human heart—a place where emotions dance, love flourishes, and the profound and the subtle intertwine like threads in a tapestry of life. This collection of poems, aptly titled "Whispers in Blue," invites you to explore the vast spectrum of human feelings and experiences, each verse a reflection of moments that have touched the core of our existence.

In these poems, you will find the joy of love, the ache of loss, the thrill of discovery, and the solace of reflection. Just as the heart has its own rhythms and melodies, so too do these verses, resonating with the myriad emotions that shape our lives.

I invite you to immerse yourself in these pages, to let the verses stir your own heart, and to discover the beauty that can be found in the complex interplay of our emotions. May these poems resonate with your own experiences, evoke memories, and perhaps even inspire you to explore the depths of your own heart's poetry.

With love and gratitude,
Soumya Varma

Frozen

There is nothing a warm heart cannot melt,
yet it thrives so hard to survive!
It could piece together a broken soul
and then be bidden goodbye.
It would gently wipe the endless tears,
feel the pain and battle the fears;
Just to be left in solitude
whilst fighting its own scrimmage.
Even then, when it comes with open arms,
yearning a caress in despair;
Shun you don't with your touch of ice
Fear this Anna might never reprise!

This too shall pass!

As we cope to live in a world,
we never so dreamt.
As we bear, kids play and grow,
in a reality quite distant.
As dear ones strangely depart,
without tears and goodbyes.
As our eyes learn to smile and laugh,
behind a new disguise.
As we nervously cling to hope,
on the path of truth and white lies.
As we slowly grow in love,
with elbow nudges, air kisses.

Let us not miss to see, we've made it this far
Once braved our secret demons
Even found beauty in old scars.
These are but new shades of blue and
like every storm, this too shall pass!

Just a child

Hey little boy, across the street
I wonder what took away your innocent dream.
I search for a twinkle in your deep eyes,
I hear no laughter, only a sad smile.

Hey little boy, across the street
I wonder what made you ride the tide.
I see the tender shoulders lead a fleet,
I yearn to see a carefree hop in your stride

Hey little boy, across the street
I wish, for a day, I could take your place
Let you spread your wings and fly
Let you laugh, let you cry
Then gently whisper in your ear
"You are just a child and it's all okay"!!

Dear Departed

*When the break of dawn chimed with your warm
wish
When we spoke for hours and felt nothing amiss
When you would cherish the days gone by
While you lost a few, yet few stood by
It was just another day!*

*When I heard you say the sound of my name
When I brushed your worries finding them lame
When our laughter and tears were at times
insane
When the distance between us was not a pain
It was just another day!*

*The day breaks with a silence now
Holding back my tears somehow
Our precious memories I'm holding tight
Being miles away doesn't feel right
You left so sudden, I had more to say
It sure will never be the same day!*

Values

No matter how vital my existence be deemed,
an adhering soul, be honored and pleased;
I know not many who pursue me for real,
neither my dweller, but on reel.

I ain't a guest that comes with age,
rather, a tenant 'with the package'.
Am shooed am booed by the rest,
and hated for the baggage I load to test.

I'd rather live within the quotes on the wall;
Short enough for a rolling eyeball!
Be buried so deep never to rise,
Fastening the shackles to reprise!

Helpless

I see a wounded creature,
dying in its own dark thoughts;
a thousand needles prick me through
bleeding me to drought.

I see it struggling in despair,
trying hard for a self-repair;
long I stretch my arms in help,
not realizing it's too far to get.

I weep! I cry! I scream! I fray!
letting my helplessness go further stray;
Alas! a hope is all I need,
that at least He will help it lead.

Conscience of the homemaker

I wonder a single day of the week,
Could start with a longer duration of sleep!
As my brutal conscience comes to prick,
I'm up on my feet with barely a wink.

It would be a relief if cooking could be skipped,
Better still, if the three course could be picked!
But no, the inner voice has to speak loud
and there this Nigella's bite is spread out.

Am sure a few calories could be lost
If I tossed out the left over for no cost.
Alas! I am pricked by the thought of the
'foodless'
I go gulping it, of course it's mindless.

I secretly wish that some fine day,
I could stop falling to the voice's prey,
The inner turmoil I would successfully fray
Hopefully before my hair turns grey!

Desire

Oh!! they call me 'desire'
'Coz I can burn like a fire,
Charring to death the wisdom taught
Adding fuel to the devilish thought.

'Tis better not to deserve me
Better still, not to yearn for me,
Keep trust on your principles
But...expect me, and you get caught!

I show you all the bliss
I can show you, all that you miss,
But 'tis you, who has to work
And shun away from this jerk!

You make a move blindfold
Falling for my magnetic hold,
I assure to mesmerize you
But…your guilt'll never forgive you

And if you do overcome me
Mark my word you win me
I then come searching for you
Making all your dreams come true!!

Contentment

Do we give a second thought
why supply maybe low, but demands ever high?
Why there is always more to be bought
No matter the price being sky-high?

It's not just the tangibles that we crave,
There is fame, power and success entail;
which are never fulfilled till the grave,
even if in giving completeness, they fail.

It's good to weigh the pros and cons,
Of a life more materialistic than happy.
As the quest for more is ever on,
Though all could be gone in a jiffy!

It's for both the Mars and Venus,
to know and give a deep thought;
that Contentment never comes to us
It has to be wisely sought!

Awakening

A smooth 'n' tender leaf I was
Entered this world through wet mass,
Grew up with the sun and its light
Swaying 'n' playing with no plight.

My veins built stronger and so did I
I held to my roots firm with pride,
I spent my time playing with the breeze
As it trespassed me buzzing with ease.

With days it became my new routine
Fondling with the waft as a teen.
Touching and feeling its cold 'n' warmth
Losing myself in its seductive swathe.

But one sad day, this dear friend
Hit me as a strong wind!!
Tossing 'n' turning I fought it real far
But it plucked 'n' threw me Oh! quite hard.

Speechless I lay as it took me away
Dumbstruck I was, had nothing to say.
Why was my trust fast crumbling
This was such a rude awakening!

Nothing more…

When the gloomy clouds of sorrow,
Trespass my heart like an arrow;
I need you beside me, dear friend,
I ask for nothing more…

When the lightning of danger,
Try an attack on my tender soul;
I need your palm to pat my head,
I ask for nothing more…

When the loud thunders of fear,
Echo around my soft ears;
I need your hand to hold it tight,
I ask for nothing more…

When the rains of my inner grief,
Start pouring down until relief;
I need your shoulder to lie on,
I ask for nothing more…

And when a rare rainbow of happiness,
Spreads its spell on my sadness;
I need that affectionate caress from you,
I ask for nothing more…

The Cry Within

Deep within the woods of my soul, so dry
I often hear a feeble cry,
Who am I? Who am I?

The angel within spreads her wings,
Says, you are living the dream dear queen,
With goodwill, loving kins and siblings,
The feathers in your cap are an inkling

I now hear a skeptical cry,
It's a lie! It's a lie!

The human within rises to its feet,
Reminds me my failures and defeats,
Tells me, my crisis I'll hardly meet
Adding fuel to the burning heat.

I now hear a painful cry,
Is that me? Is that me?

Oh! the devil storms in so fast!
Proliferating further the hollowness half-cast.
Declares my identity is a past,
You are nowhere, you are the last.

I now hear a mournful cry,
Could it be? Could it be?

Hush this cry, listen to me
These are but colours, life paints on me,
and till the last drop vanishes
Why bother whoever 'me' maybe??

Death

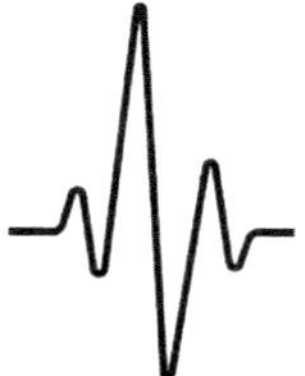

Death, for a few, is the liberation of soul,
While some say, it is life's final call.

When a newborn's heart stops, it's a tragedy,
A musician's demise, leaves behind the melody.

When a young life is lost, it creates agony,
An old man's instead, completes life's journey.

A politician's last breath, demands national
grievance,
A common man's loss, sadly, makes no
difference.

Take a closer look at these from the other side,
And know that it's a fact that man has to abide.

Be it early, be it sudden or be it the end of a
race,
Let's not define death with a phrase or a face.

Accept this pearl of wisdom in turn,
'DEATH', you need no longer spurn.

How we met

I met a sweet soul, on a chill cold night
Wrapped in a woolen shawl, with eyes closed
tight.
She welcomed me with a warm smile
Followed with an "intro" in her own style.
We talked and we laughed across a mile
And took a silent pause for a short while.
Never once I thought, my space I'll have to
share
With this embodiment of creativity, that has a
singing flair.
Today we have come a long way so soon
Oh! I never thought; 'that night out' could be
such a BOON!

A Blossom in my life

Fingers crossed, I stood at the door;
Waiting for a cry, then a loud uproar.
Yes!! I heard it!! Oh my sweet princess was
born;
Wrapped up in white, to bring happiness
unbound.

Within months, my sweetie, learnt to look into
my eyes,
And kept me awake with her smiles & whines,
till 'twas sunrise;
At times I was a horse, for her to take a ride;
At times "the strongest dad", in whom she took
pride.

Within years, my little angel, grew into a young lady;
With beauty and a sober charm, driving guys crazy.
An urge grew within me, to guard her from everyone's sight;
I now found a new reason, for spending sleepless nights.

Today at this threshold, I have to bid her adieu;
As she unites with her prince charming, for a life all new.
I struggle to hold back the lump in my throat,
And my old eyes in tears, start to float.

I gift you a priceless possession my dear son-in-law;
Whom you shall never hurt, that's the line I draw.
With all my prayers and blessings galore;
I soon hope to see you son with fingers crossed at a door.

Head Vs Heart

Sat at my window, with the whiff of petrichor
as the raindrops brushed through a rainbow,
my heart yearned… to step out, soak and play
but alas! the head said, 'Why don't you stay?'
Back I stepped, giving in to the voice…

Standing at my door, with a broken heart
bidding goodbye to the one not meant to be
apart,
my heart yearned… hold that hand, don't let go
but alas! the head said, 'What if it only gives
sorrow?'
Back I stepped, having no choice…

Stuck at the cross gate, of work and life
pulled both ways of passion and pride,
my heart yearned…to chase my dreams and fly
but alas! the head said, 'That doesn't comply'.
Back I stepped, yet again, to pay the price…

Sipping my coffee on the couch one day
my head took pride in life's fullness and gay.
That moment my heart with sarcasm smiled
My dear friend, "Happiness you can never
define"!

Guess what?

Bet am hot, bet am sexy
could be simple or even tacky
bewilder you may, that's my speciality
'coz I behold such an entity.

Resist you can't my precious secret
my touch can make even a macho fret
if he does manage to hack this net
I promise a sight he'd never regret

Am secular, my support is a miracle
now does the name 'Joey' ring a bell?
an optimist, my cup's always full
trust me this poem ain't no bull!!

Humour

You think I'm a mere state of mind
Hey! I'm much more than that.
A secret doctor with a healing touch
who can tickle many a different part.

I mostly appeal to the human heart
unblocking all the stress.
I wipe those wrinkles off your face
when you chuckle, giggle or laugh.

Funnily at times I do go rogue
and end up hurting your tummy.
With teary eyes and a laughter riot
that at times could sound wheezy.

I seldom come in a bad shape
Or unintentionally leave a poor taste,
But you sure could take a chill pill
and try to simply 'humour me'!!!

F(u)riend

When our eyes first met, you cutely tilted your
head,
then came bolting to sniff my feet.
When I called your name, you wagged your tail,
and wouldn't stop jumping for a treat.

It felt very strange to be this close,
Silly me, I wonder what was I scared of!
I was amazed, by your naughty little tricks;
Seeing your ears up on guard, ever so quick.

I was thrilled to give you a nice neck rub
and be followed around like a bub.
With your paws on my lap, that Friday night
Dear Scruffy, it was pure love at first sight!!

If Animals and Birds are educated (Unedited - where it all began)*

In my heart thoughts arise
What'll happen if animals and birds become wise?
World will be under their rule
Life will shine like a moon
They will teach us not to be wild
Instead, they will make us mild.

They won't take revenge for our ill-treatment
'Coz they know love is an ointment
Jungle will be an advanced world
Full of educated animals and birds
Politeness will be their weapon
'Live and let live' will be their slogan

They will follow modern civilization
And help everyone in every situation
They will decorate the physical feature
Work together and save our beautiful nature
Now I feel it'll be so nice
If animals and birds too become wise.

*(This was the very first poem I wrote in school when my English teacher gave us a surprise writing challenge one day)

Made in heaven

It was not when you went down on a knee
nor when you slid the ring.
It was not when I walked down the aisle
nor when I said 'I do'.
It was not when we danced together
nor when we exchanged the vows.
Two humans in a wedding lock
are not made in heaven by default.

It is when we speak through tiny gestures
and hold our hands together.
It is when we read each other's minds
and choose to hold our silence.
It is when we express mutual love and care
and sail through rough times.
Two humans and a promise of companionship
is what truly makes it happen.